Scott Foresman

Accelerating English Language Learning

Newcomer Book B

Authors

Anna Uhl Chamot
Jim Cummins
Carolyn Kessler
J. Michael O'Malley
Lily Wong Fillmore

Consultant

George González

Writers

Ellen Balla
Carolyn Grigsby

ISBN 0-13-027537-9
Copyright © 2001, 1997 Scott, Foresman and Company
All Rights Reserved. Printed in the United States of America.
This publication is protected by Copyright and permission should be obtained
from the publisher prior to any prohibited reproduction, storage in a retrieval
system, or transmission in any form or by any means, electronic, mechanical,
photocopying, recording, or otherwise. For information regarding permission,
write to:
Pearson Education
10 Bank Street, White Plains, NY 10606

6 7 8 9 10-WC-05 04 03 02

TABLE OF CONTENTS

TABLE OF CONTENTS

7

Lesson Seven: Working at School 25

- to identify/say action verbs
- to practice the present-progressive tense
- to review classroom objects
- to talk/write about school activities
- to make connections

8

Lesson Eight • Lunchtime 29

- to identify/say foods
- to express preferences
- to identify/say meals
- to review time
- to survey classmates

9

Lesson Nine • After School 33

- to identify/say action verbs
- to practice the present-progressive tense
- to express preferences
- to talk about after-school activities
- to survey classmates

10

Lesson Ten • My Neighborhood 37

- to identify/say neighborhood places
- to review action verbs
- to identify/say directions
- to practice the present-progressive tense
- to make a map

Tell what you know.

Good-by, Ana.

Hi. My name is Alan.

Hi. I'm Lara. This is Josie.

Say the words.

desk

table

book

notebook

chair

pencil

pen

marker

paper

Say the numbers. Read the words.

	0	zero
	1	one
	2	two
	3	three
	4	four
	5	five
	6	six
	7	seven
	8	eight
	9	nine
	10	ten

How many? Count the items.

I have two notebooks.

I have one notebook.

Items	desk 1	+	desk 2	=	how many?
notebooks	2	+	1	=	3
1. pencils		+		=	
2. books		+		=	
3. markers		+		=	

Play the game.  page 41

Count. Write the number.

1.  + = _____

2.  +  = _____

3.  +  = _____

Circle the picture.

1. desk 	2. pencil
3. table	4. notebook
5. marker	6. book

Write the number.

I have _____ books.

I have _____ pencils.

I have _____ notebooks.

I have one book. What do you have?

Tell what you know.

What's your address?

47 Elm Street, Los Angeles, California 90027.

What's your phone number?

(213) 555-7846.

Look at the pictures. Say the words.

letter   address

Joe Hererra
47 Elm Street
Los Angeles, CA 90027

city   state   zip code

house

street

(213)555-7846

area code   phone number   phone

Say the alphabet.

Aa Bb Cc Dd Ee Ff Gg Hh Ii
Jj Kk Ll Mm Nn Oo Pp Qq Rr
Ss Tt Uu Vv Ww Xx Yy Zz

Write your name. Spell it.

My name is _____.

> My name is Kenji. K-e-n-j-i.

Kenji

Write your phone number.

Ask a partner.

> My phone number is (312) 555-7307. What's your phone number?

My phone number is

(_____)_____.

My friend's phone number is

(_____)_____.

Send a letter to a friend.

Write the address.

> 17 Maple Street, Miami, Florida 33143

> What's your address?

Luis Mendoza
17 Maple Street
Miami, Florida
33143

Read the rhyme with a partner.

Say the letters A, B, C.

Point to D, E, F, and G.

Write an X on H, I, J.

Say and write the letter K. ____

Circle L, M, N, O, P.

Color Q, R, S, and T.

Write the letters U and V. ____ ____

Draw a line through W, X, Y, Z.

N	Z	P	H
F	A	D	
K	I	Q	S
W	B	G	
M	R	X	T
Y	J	U	O
C	E	V	L

Make a phone book. page 43

Ask.

What's your phone number?

Write.

Cut.

Staple.

Circle the word.

1.		house phone	2.	crayon pen
3.		phone number phone	4.	book chair

Write the letters.

a b ___ d e f ___ h i j ___ l m ___

___ p q ___ s ___ u v w ___ y z

Write your phone number.

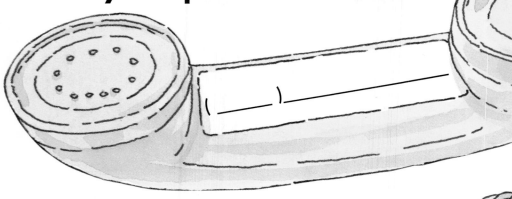

(_____) _____

I can.

☐ I can say my name and address.
☐ I can say my area code and phone number.
☐ I can say the alphabet.

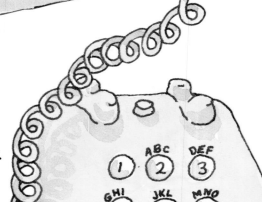

Tell what you know.

Say the times.

It's twelve o'clock.

It's three o'clock.

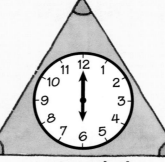

It's six o'clock.

It's nine o'clock.

Say the numbers.

11	12	13	14	15	16
eleven	twelve	thirteen	fourteen	fifteen	sixteen

17	18	19	20	21
seventeen	eighteen	nineteen	twenty	twenty-one

Say the colors.

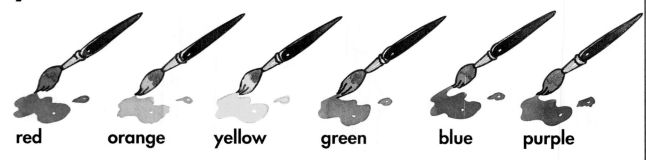

red   **orange**   **yellow**   **green**   **blue**   **purple**

Say the shapes.

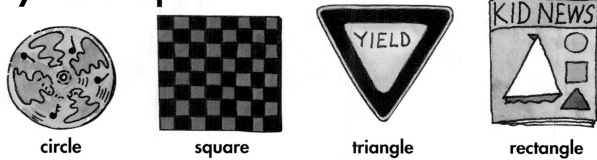

circle   square   triangle   rectangle

Find the shapes in your classroom.

Work with a partner.

Item	Shape
clock	*circle*
1.	
2.	
3.	

Circle the word.

1.		orange yellow red	2.		green purple blue
3.		orange red blue	4.		green yellow blue

Color the shapes. Make a pattern.

pattern

1.

2.

3.

Write the numbers. Say the times.

_8:00_   1. _____   2. _____   3. _____   4. _____

Play bingo. page 45

Write the times.

1. _____ 2. _____ 3. _____ 4. _____ 5. _____

Circle the word.

1.		red blue yellow	2. 	orange blue red
3.		yellow blue orange	4.	green orange yellow

Color the shapes. Make a pattern.

1.

2.

3.

I can. ✓

☐ I can tell time.

☐ I can say   .   ☐ I can say   .

☐ I can count to 21.

Tell what you know.

Say the days of the week.

Sunday	Monday	Tuesday	Wednesday	Thursday	Friday	Saturday
1	2	3	4	5	6	7

Say the months of the year.

JANUARY · FEBRUARY · MARCH · APRIL
MAY · JUNE · JULY · AUGUST
SEPTEMBER · OCTOBER · NOVEMBER · DECEMBER

Look at the pictures. Put them in order.

1. They have art on Wednesday.

2. They have music on Tuesday.

3. They have library on Friday.

Circle the word.

1. **Tuesday, Wednesday, _____ , Friday**

   Monday   Sunday   Thursday   Saturday

2. **Monday, _____ , Wednesday, Thursday**

   Sunday   Friday   Tuesday   Saturday

3. **January, _____ , March, April**

   July   May   February   December

4. **March, April, May, _____**

   January   February   June   August

When do you have class?
Work with a partner.

Class	Day	My Partner's Class	Day
1.		1.	
2.		2.	
3.		3.	

Make a class calendar. page 47

Cut.   Paste.   Write.   Draw.

What holidays do you know?
Write them on the class calendar. Work with a partner.

Circle the word.

1. **Sunday, _____ , Tuesday, Wednesday**

   Friday   Thursday   Saturday   Monday

2. **Tuesday, Wednesday, _____ , Friday**

   Monday   Friday   Thursday   Saturday

3. **May, June, _____ , August**

   August   December   January   July

4. **February, March, April, _____**

   August   June   May   February

Write about yourself.

I have art on _____ .

I have music on _____ .

My favorite subject is _____ .

I can.

☐ I can say the days of the week.
☐ I can say the months of the year.
☐ I can say subject names.
☐ I can talk about my schedule.

Tell what you know.

This is the classroom.

This is the nurse's office.

This is the girls' rest room.

This is my school.

This is the office.

PRINCIPAL

This is the library.

LIBRARIAN

What time is it? Say the times.

It's one thirty.

It's three thirty.

3:30

It's six thirty.

9:30

It's nine thirty.

Who's this? Say the names.

principal

teacher

librarian

student

secretary

Draw a line from the people to the places.

Name the people and places.

1.

2.

3.

a.

b.

c.

Draw the times.

It's two thirty.		1. It's eleven thirty.	
2. It's nine thirty.		3. It's four thirty.	

Do the puzzle.

Write the words you know first.

Across →

1. 2.

3. 4.

Down ↓

5.

6.

7. PRINCIPAL

Crossword puzzle:

6 Down: s e c r e t a r y

Write a story. ✂ page 49

Tell it to a partner.

My name is _____ .

I _____ .

My name is Ana. I go to school at 8:30.

Who are the people in your school? Write.

My English teacher's name is _____ .

My principal's name is _____ .

The librarian's name is _____ .

Draw the times.

1. It's three thirty.   2. It's one thirty.   3. It's five thirty.   4. It's four thirty.

Draw a line from the people to the places.

1.    a.

2.    b.

3.    c.

I can. ✔

☐ I can tell time.

☐ I can name the people in my school.

Tell what you know.

It's sunny. What are you wearing today?

I'm wearing shorts and a T-shirt.

It's rainy. What are you wearing?

I'm wearing pants, a sweater, and a raincoat.

Say the words.

 pants

 T-shirt

 raincoat

 backpack

 shorts

shoes

umbrella

 dress

jacket

 sweater

Say the words.

It's rainy.

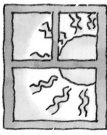

It's sunny.

It's windy.

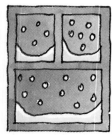

It's snowy.

It's cloudy.

Draw a line from the weather to the clothes.

It's snowy.

It's rainy.

It's sunny.

scarf

umbrella

raincoat

sandals

shorts

jacket

hat

T-shirt

Circle the word.

1.		pants shorts jacket	2.		hat T-shirt sandals
3.		raincoat umbrella scarf	4.		T-shirt shorts dress

Read the descriptions with a partner.

Hi! My name is Maria. I'm wearing a yellow shirt, brown pants, and white shoes. I have an orange jacket.

Hi! My name is Chris. I'm wearing a green sweater, blue pants, and black shoes. I have a green backpack.

Practice with a partner.

I'm wearing a green shirt, black pants, and brown shoes. I have a red jacket. What are you wearing?

I'm wearing a blue dress and black shoes. I have a red backpack.

Draw and write your own description.
Read it to a friend.

Hi! My name is _____.

I'm wearing _____,

_____, and _____.

I have a _____.

Play the matching game. ✂ page 51

It's sunny. I'm wearing shorts.

It's rainy. I have an umbrella.

match

Draw the clothes.

1.

green jacket

2.

blue pants

3.

red T-shirt

Write the weather.

1.

2.

3.

It's _____ .   It's _____ .   It's _____ .

I can. ✔

☐ I can say the names of clothing.
☐ I can say the weather.
☐ I can talk about my clothes.

Tell what you know.

> What are you doing?

> I'm working on the computer.

Say the words.

multiplying

measuring

painting

reading

dividing

working on the computer

writing

Say the words.

adding

subtracting

drawing

kicking the ball

singing

running

playing soccer

making a map

Draw the pictures. Say the words.

1.

I'm multiplying.

2.

I'm drawing.

3.

I'm playing soccer.

Practice with a partner.

What are you doing?

I'm writing a story.

Draw lines from the people to the items.

What do they need?

1.  I'm dividing.

2.  I'm painting.

3.  I'm measuring.

4.  I'm playing soccer.

5.  I'm reading.

a.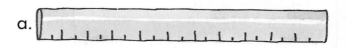

b.

c.

d.

e.

Act it out. Have a partner guess.  page 53

Reading?

Reading

Read the story.

Circle the word.

1. 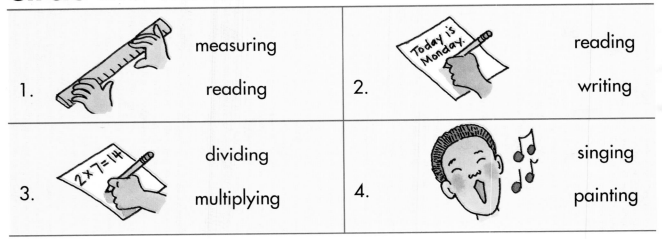	measuring reading	2.	reading writing
3.	dividing multiplying	4.	singing painting

Write the words.

1.

I'm _____.

2.

I'm _____.

3.

I'm _____.

I can.

☐ I can read and write about what I do at school.
☐ I can talk about what I do at school.

Tell what you know.

What do you like to eat?

I like to eat apples.

Say the words.

apple   banana   juice   sandwich   grapes

milk   taco   pizza   cookie

Say the words.

corn

chicken

broccoli

rice

potato

bread

ice cream

hamburger

Draw pictures. Write the words.

What do you like to eat?

1.

I like to eat _____.

2.

I like to eat _____.

3.

I like to eat _____.

4.

I like to eat _____.

Ask your friends. Take a survey.

Name	Likes To Eat
Tina	pizza
1.	
2.	
3.	

What do you like to eat?

I like to eat pizza.

Read the Story.

For breakfast, I like to eat cereal, toast, and an orange. I like to drink juice.

For lunch, I like to eat a sandwich, an apple, and cookies. I like to drink milk.

For dinner, I like to eat chicken, rice, and salad. I like to drink milk.

Draw a picture. Write the words.

What do you like?

For _____,

I like to eat _____,

_____, and

_____.

I like to drink _____.

Make a meal. page 55

Cut.

Choose.

Glue.

Write.

Draw the food.

1.	2.	3.	4.
apple	sandwich	pizza	banana

Write the words.

1. _____
2. _____
3. _____
4. _____

Write. Use the words in the box.

breakfast

lunch

dinner

1. _____
2. _____
3. _____

I can. ✔

☐ I can say the names of food.

☐ I can say what I like to eat.

☐ I can write about the foods I like.

☐ I can ask my friends what they like.

Tell what you know.

I like to do my homework.

What do you like to do after school?

I like to eat a snack.

I like to play soccer.

I like to talk to my friends.

I like to play the piano.

Say the words.

read a book

play basketball

clean my room

listen to music

go to the library

ride my bike

Practice with a friend.

Ask your friends. Take a survey.

Name	Likes to
Mike	listen to music
1.	
2.	
3.	

Draw pictures. Write the words.
What do you like to do after school?

1.

First I _____

_____.

2.

Then I _____

_____.

3.

Then I _____

_____.

Read the sentences.

She's doing her homework.

He's playing soccer.

He's reading a book.

She's eating a snack.

Circle the sentences.

What are they doing?

1. He's riding a bike. He's playing soccer.	2.  She's reading a book. She's playing the piano.
3.  He's eating a snack. He's doing his homework.	4.  She's listening to music. She's talking to her friends.

Make a book. page 57

Write sentences.

Cut and staple the pages.

Read it to a friend.

Draw pictures.
What are they doing?

1. He's reading a book.	2. She's playing basketball.
3. She's eating a snack.	4. He's doing his homework.

Write the sentences.

She's playing the piano.

1. _____.

2. _____.

3. _____.

I can. ✔

☐ I can talk about what I do after school.

☐ I can write about what I do after school.

☐ I can ask my friends what they do after school.

☐ I can write about what my friends do after school.

Tell what you know.

Where are you going?

I'm going to the library.

PUBLIC LIBRARY

READ!

What are you doing at the library?

I'm checking out a book.

PUBLIC LIBRARY

READ!

Say the words.

library

post office

supermarket

bus stop

laundromat

park

mall

movie theater

Circle the word.

1.

park

post office

mall

2.

supermarket

bus stop

park

3.

laundromat

library

post office

Say the words.

checking out a book

mailing a letter

buying food

waiting for a bus

washing clothes

playing basketball

shopping at the mall

watching a movie

Practice with a friend.

Say the directions.

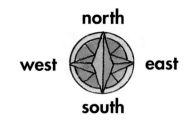

Look at the map. Write the directions.
Which way?

Which way to the school?   *Go north.*

Which way to the post office?   1. Go _____.

Which way to the library?   2. Go _____.

Which way to the police station?   3. Go _____.

Make a map. ✂ page 59

Cut out the places.

Glue places on the map.

Show it to a friend.

Write the directions.

_____

_____ _____

_____

Circle the sentence.

What are they doing?

1.

   They're shopping.

   They're mailing a letter.

   They're washing clothes.

2.

   They're playing basketball.

   They're checking out books.

   They're buying food.

3.

   She's watching a movie.

   She's buying food.

   She's washing clothes.

4.

   He's waiting for a bus.

   He's mailing a letter.

   He's shopping.

I can.

☐ I can talk about places in my neighborhood.

☐ I can write about places in my neighborhood.

☐ I can say and write directions.

☐ I can make a map.

Cut. Fasten. Spin.

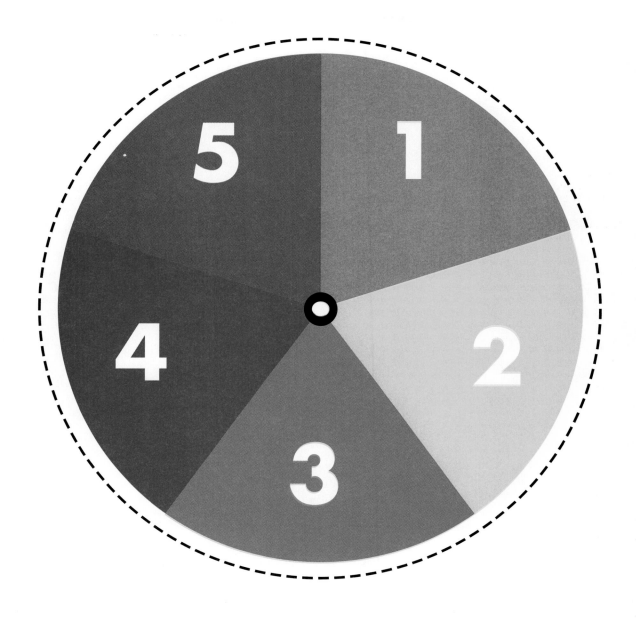

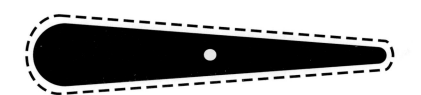

Cut out the pages to the phone book.

Name _____ Phone Number _____

Name _____ Phone Number _____

Name _____ Phone Number _____

Name _____ Phone Number _____

Name _____ Phone Number _____

Name _____ Phone Number _____

Name _____ Phone Number _____

Name _____ Phone Number _____

Cut out the clocks. Play bingo.

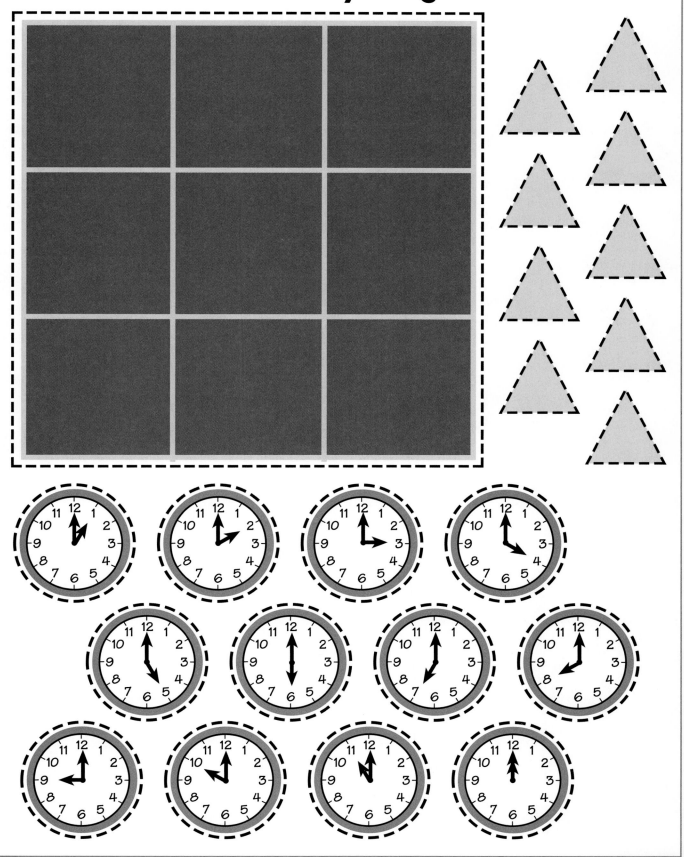

Cut out the calendar.

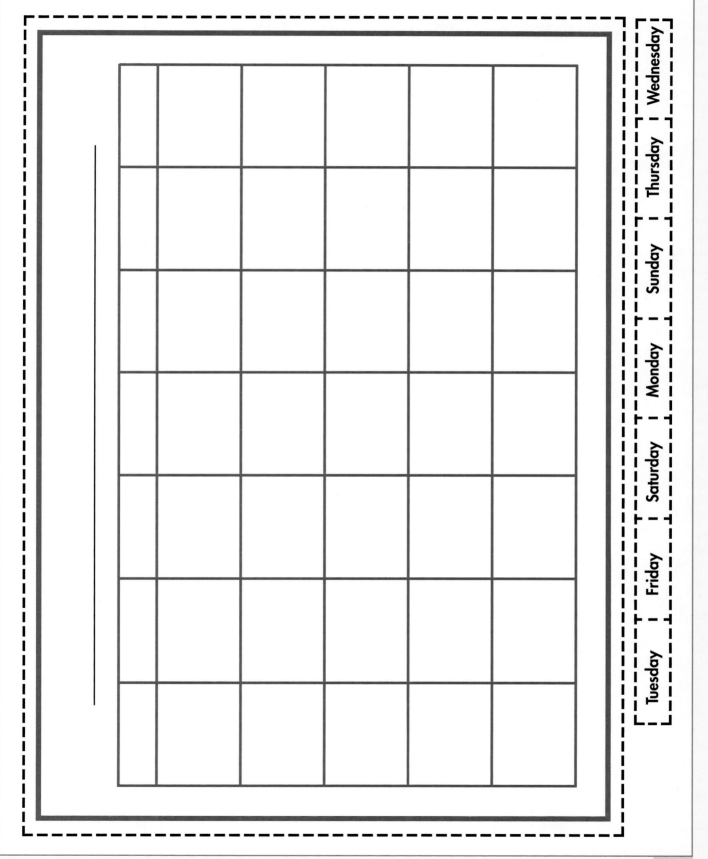

Draw times. Cut out the pictures.

Sunday	Monday	Tuesday	Wednesday
Thursday	Friday	Saturday	

Cut out the cards.
Match the weather and clothes.

Cut out the cards. Act them out.

multiplying

dividing

adding

subtracting

singing

working on the computer

writing

measuring

kicking a ball

painting

reading

playing basketball

Cut. Make a meal. Write about it.

Cut out the pages. Make a book.

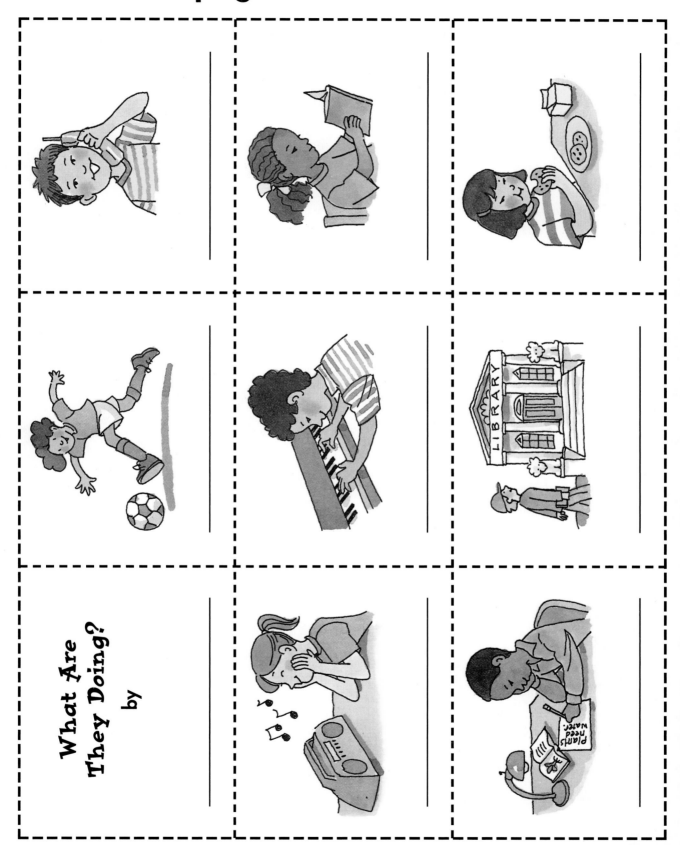

What Are
They Doing?
by

Cut. Make a map. Show it to a friend.

Illustrations by Diane Paterson and George Ulrich